OBJECTIONS

Category: Business & Economics

ISBN 978-1-105-22302-0

©2017 by Bob Oros Publishing

Standard Copyright License

Author: Bob Oros

Description: You will learn how to carefully remove every objection that a customer presents to you as a reason why they are not interested in buying. This book will show you how to overcome all the objections that have ever been presented from a variety of customers and under numerous conditions.

Key words: follow up

ISBN 978-1-105-22302-0

9 781105 223020

90000

Objections

Remove every roadblock to the sale

Smoke screen objections

Do any of these sound familiar?

I have too many suppliers already.

I really don't like your company.

We've been doing all right without you.

I'm tied up in a supplier contract.

I'm happy with my present supplier.

You don't carry a full line.

I'm not interested at this time.

See me in a couple of months.

I hear your company is having problems.

Business is down.

Why will someone continue to buy from a sales person when it is obvious they are not happy with the service, price or quality? The reason is that the buyer is comfortable dealing with the sales person and company he or she is buying from. To make a change requires assurances that you will be able to handle their business.

Many times in the buyers mind it is easier to stay with their current supplier even if the prices and delivery are not exactly as they would like. That is why they have at least five objections that you must overcome before they feel sure enough to give you their business.

The best response to smoke screen objections is to be sincerely glad they brought it up. When answering "smoke screen" objections the normal response is to agree with the objection, however, the best response is to say "I'm glad you brought that up!" And then ask a question.

This is a non-confrontational approach. When you do it sincerely you will come across with real concern for your customer.

How would you handle these common objections? I have too many suppliers already. I really don't like your company. We've been doing all right without you. I'm tied up in supplier contract. I'm happy with my present supplier. You don't carry a full line. I'm not interested at this time. See me in a couple of months. I hear your company is having problems. Business is down.

When answering these "smoke screen" objections the normal response is to agree with the objection, however, an excellent response is to say "I'm glad you brought that up!" And then ask a question. For example:

"I don't like your company". Response: "I'm glad you brought that up. It sounds to me like someone must have done something in the past and it is Important that we get honest feedback about our products and services. What exactly is it that you don't like about our company?"

"I have too many suppliers already". Response: "I'm glad you brought that up. That certainly can be a problem, how many is too many?" "I may be able to help you consolidate," etc.

"You don't carry the items I need". Response: "I'm glad you brought that up. Would you mind telling me which items you are referring to?"

Often we can get the prospect to answer his own objection or to admit that it is not a valid objection. To let the prospect answer his own objection you just let them talk.. Maybe he will answer his own objection. In any event, he will lower his blood pressure. You may say, for example, "I am interested in why you say that, Mr. Smith. I wish you would explain it to me more fully." You may merely ask him, "Why do you believe that?" If, as so often happens, the objection is not a valid one and the prospect has at best only a half-baked idea of what he is talking about, he will usually flounder around a while and end by admitting that the matter is of no importance.

When answering "smoke screen" objections the normal response is to agree with the objection, however, the best response is to say "I'm glad you brought that up!" And then ask a question.

Ask for the price you would like to get

The reason sales people hesitate to ask for what they want is fear of rejection.

Don't fear rejection.

Don't worry about making the customer angry.

Don't be immobilized by your own timidity.

Don't have negative thoughts that will set you up for failure.

"They'll never give up their current supplier and buy form me, so there's no point in even asking."

If you don't make the request the customer is already ahead!

You've made things easy for them! They made the pitch and you bought it!

You've eliminated the possibility that they might say yes or agree to a compromise solution that is equally desirable.

If you are dealing with a person who is not afraid to ask for what they want and you have only a vague idea of what you want, it is like going into a gun fight with no bullets in your gun.

Set your sights high. When you ask for a higher price you allow yourself room to move--trading for other items in the sale you might want during the presentation.

The essence of selling is to make your request loud and clear so the customer hears it.

Don't be afraid to do just that. Don't be embarrassed to ask for the business.

A price buyer technique

Retail stores often advertise fabulous but fake bargains just to get you to come in so they can sell you something more expensive. This scheme is commonly referred to as "bait and switch."

It is simple enough: they advertise some item at a price low enough to lure you into the store. But here is the switch: the advertised item is not for sale. The salespeople may give you any number of reasons why you cannot or should not buy it.

"There are not any left. . ."

"Many customers who bought it are dissatisfied . . ."

"The product is not any good . . ."

"You cannot get delivery for six months . . ."

The truth is that these salespeople never had any intention of selling the advertised special. They kill your desire to buy it and instead try to get you to buy the item they had in mind from the beginning.

"Bait and switch" is an unfair practice and is against the law. Although you cannot always spot bait ads in advance or know that the switch is going to follow, there are a few steps you can take to avoid the trap.

First, realize that a good salesperson may try to persuade you to buy a better quality item or a different brand with more features at a higher price. There is nothing illegal or unethical about this. The important thing is that you are given a choice without undue pressure.

Keep in mind that if a product or service is advertised at a price that seems too good to be true, this may be a bait ad. Then, if the merchant refuses to show you the advertised item, to take orders for it or deliver it within a reasonable time, disparages it, or demonstrates a defective sample of it, take this as a sign that you are probably being "switched."

For example: You go into a store to buy a computer you saw advertised. It was out of stock, but when a salesperson tells you a faster model is available for an additional $100, you purchased it because it was available immediately.

The deliberate use of stock outages of a featured, low-price bait brand in hope of persuading customers to switch to a more profitable substitute brand is a form of bait and switch.

Buyers use this by asking for a price on a large quantity and then order a smaller quantity trying to get you to agree to your first price.

Buyers sometimes use the bait and switch by asking for a price on a large quantity and then order a smaller quantity trying to get you to agree to your first price.

A common mistake

If everyone is always beating you up on price, maybe it is because of the way you are presenting it. Presenting your price with implied flexibility should be used as a tool, not as the normal way you present it.

For example, if someone asks for a price on 10 cases of a product you are selling, you would not want to say; "somewhere around $1.49" if the price was, in fact, $1.49. By using the term "somewhere around" you have opened the door for the buyer to assume the price is flexible.

State the price firmly like you mean it. Many people don't state the price firmly and unknowingly open up the door for the buyer to start working on their price. Sometime the person presenting the price will do so giving a range rather that a firm price.

For example: "The price is between thirty five and forty dollars per case." This response signals a lack of confidence in the price quoted and encourages the customer to start working down the price not from forty dollars, but from thirty five dollars.

Practice delivering your price with a tone of confidence. Deliver it with the same conviction that you would use to give someone your phone number.

"What are the last four digits of your phone number?"

5197 - Not "between 5197 and 5200".

What month were you born?

October - Not "somewhere between September and November".

If you signal with words such as "about" or "roughly,'" the buyer will take this to mean that you can go lower. If you do imply flexibility follow the other rule of selling - ask for more than you expect to get, because you may need the room.

Flexibility is a tool you can use - sometimes you might want to imply a certain degree of flexibility.

For example. Let's say a customer is looking for 100 cases of your product. You know that the customer has shopped around for a couple of other quotes. Giving your price too firmly may cause you to lose the business. However, giving your highest price and slightly implying that you are willing to work with the customer will open the door to a possible sale that would otherwise be lost.

But remember - flexibility is a tool - a strategy to use when the situation calls for it.

If everyone is always beating you up on price, maybe it is because of the way you are presenting it. Presenting your price with implied flexibility should be used as a tool, not as the normal way you present it.

Five times more for an invention

An experienced buyer will very seldom, if ever, accept your first price. An experienced seller knows this and always presents a price higher than they expect to get.

A buyer will feel like they are not doing their job if they don't get a sales person to move down a little on price. As a seller, if you don't give them a price reduction they will feel like you out-smarted them.

When someone asks you for a price on a single item that you know is price sensitive, try and get them to give you the price they are looking for.

For example: As you start looking up the price or waiting for your computer to boot up, you might respond with: "I'll be happy to give you a price on that, by the way, what price are you looking for?"

If you do get the buyer to tell you how much he or she is willing to pay, act slightly shocked as if their opening price is low!

"I have to admit that price is really low."

When you are selling, always start at your highest price whenever possible. No matter what the customer may say (such as "This is a one-time only offer; take it or leave it!"), don't take it! If they really want to make the purchase, they'll move from that price.

Don't be shy when you state your original price - put on a show of confidence. Amateurs almost always hesitate when giving their first price and professionals very seldom do.

The more you ask for in the beginning, the better. You're not being greedy - you're being smart. Eventually you will meet an acceptable compromise, but usually not in the beginning.

When you ask for a higher price, you can always come down. If you begin by asking for a higher price and you know you will settle for the lower price, everyone comes out a winner. If you start low you may end up having to go ever lower.

Here's an example: I was in Ft Myers Florida taking a tour of Thomas Edison's winter home and workshop. The tour guide told a story I will never forget.

Thomas Edison had invented the "Ticker Tape" machine and was in the buyer's office in New York to sell it for use in the New York Stock Exchange. The buyer asked Edison how much he wanted for it. Edison said, "How much will you give me?" The buyer said "$25,000". Edison said, "I'll take it!"

Later they were having dinner and the buyer said to Edison, "you were mighty quick to jump on that $25,000; I would have paid all the way up to $50,000." Edison said, "I would have taken $5,000.

Don't be shy when you state your original price - put on a show of confidence. Amateurs almost always hesitate

when giving their first price and professionals very
seldom do.

Shocked at your price

The best story I have ever heard is from a buyer who
claimed he could get a sales person to lower their price
without saying a word. He said he was able to perfect
his "price shock" strategy by practicing on his way to
work every morning.

What exactly is "price shock?" It is a simple facial
expression that says, "Your price seems high!" Well-
trained buyers are taught to use this strategy with exact
precision.

When a buyer is looking at your initial price they are
taught to wrinkle their forehead as if to say "you are
much higher than I expected!" This is designed to
immediately put you, the presenter, on the defensive.
The sad part is, it works most of the time. Even if you
have a close relationship with the buyer, you may

misread it as a sign that you should lower your price to get, or keep, the business.

Work on your own price shock until you can perfect it. Every time you buy something act surprised at the price. Watch closely how the seller reacts. Whenever you are given a price on anything, act slightly surprised – watch carefully how they respond. Simply say "the price seems a little high", or "I am sure this is a great product, however, your price seems a little high", or "I was thinking about buying a new boat, however, your price seems a little high!"

What about when someone is shocked at YOUR PRICE? What should your reaction be? There are four responses you can use for this powerful strategy:

1. You can be weak, give in, and lower your price. They won. This is what most buyers expect, especially from an amateur.

2. You can be shocked at their shock. This is designed to neutralize the strategy. The customer is shocked at

your price; you are shocked at their shock. Seems a little strange to use at first, until you see how well it works. This throws the shock right back at the buyer and you have now put the buyer on the defensive. Then stay silent. Do not provide an explanation. It is the buyer's turn to make the next move!

3. You can use the "Feel, Felt, Found" reply. Here is how it works: "I understand why you feel that way, everyone I talked to so far today felt the same way, until they found out that the market has gone up since last week."

4. You can justify your price rather that discount it. This is an extension of number three. "I understand why you might feel that way, everyone I talked to today felt the same way, until they found out what is included in that price." And then begin to list the additional benefits that are included, which makes the price seem smaller and smaller.

Be shocked at their shock. This is designed to neutralize the strategy. The customer is shocked at your price; you are shocked at their shock.

Higher authority

I once asked a hotel clerk for a discount and she informed me that she would have to check with the manager. She walked through the office door behind her and returned in about 10 seconds informing me that the manager said no. As I waited for the elevator I heard another guest ask for a discount – same thing – she walked to the office behind her only now I could see the entire office. The office was empty! She simply walked into the office, waited about five seconds and returned telling the guest that the manager said no!

Another good lesson learned was from a sales person in Twin Falls, Idaho. A friend of his sold a service station to someone from another country that didn't understand how we do business. The new owner would order a part from the auto supply store and then try to negotiate the price with the driver.

You may be thinking how anyone could do something like that. However, if we go into an account and are not talking to the decision maker, we are doing the same thing.

Sometimes a decision maker will use a "higher authority" to hide the fact that they are the decision maker. For example: "This agreement looks good, but I will have to run it by my committee (or wife or any other higher authority)."

If you are the one making the presentation and the presence of someone important is impossible, set a short one or two day time limit for his or her higher authority approval.

You can use this same strategy. You can start your presentation with the same question. "If I show you a program that will not only save you money on your operating expenses, but also lower your labor cost as well as increase your sales, is there any reason why you would not want to give it the go-ahead?" If the buyer has to get approval from a higher authority you will know how to tailor your presentation.

If you are making a presentation to a person who does not have authority to make the decision, the best strategy is to build up the person you are presenting. Suggest to the person that the committee is surely influenced by what he or she says. If you can get them to commit to making a "sale" to the committee, it can be embarrassing if he or she is not able to get it through for you.

Another strategy if you are selling to a buyer who has to "run it by the committee" is to ask about the possibility of making a presentation to the committee yourself. This can either call their bluff or it may present you with an opportunity to actually make a presentation to the buying committee.

When making YOUR presentation it is to your advantage to present a higher authority from which you must get approval. Even if you do have complete authority over the selling price, you may want the buyer to believe you have to get approval.

When making YOUR presentation it is to your advantage to present a higher authority from which you must get approval.

Good Guy / Bad Guy

Good guy/bad guy is taking the higher authority strategy to the next level. The good guy/bad guy can be obvious or it can be quite subtle. It can be carefully planned in advance, or people can fall into the roles naturally.

When this buying strategy is used, you might not even notice until you have become the victim. The real estate agent and client often use this method. For example, the home seller might play the bad guy, holding out for top dollar. But the seller's agent plays the good guy by showing the bad guy why the price is above market value.

Husband and wife teams often use this method too. The husband is usually the bad guy while the wife is more reasonable and sympathetic to the other side's viewpoint.

Good guy/bad guy occurs when there are two or more buyers and one is easier to get along with, provides more information, or seems more anxious to make a deal, while the other is more difficult.

I recently sold a travel trailer and was amazed at how most husbands and wives fall into these roles. The wife would make the initial call and get all the information before handing the phone over to the husband, the bad guy, to talk about the price.

We have all seen the good guy/bad guy tactics on television. A suspect is caught and interrogated. The first detective puts him under a glaring light, hits him with hard questions and roughs him up.

The tough guy leaves. In comes the nice guy who gives the suspect a cigarette and lets him relax. Soon the suspect spills all he knows.

Car dealerships are known for this. When the sales person says "I will take this to the sales manager and see if I can get this price for you", they actually make us believe they are on our side!

Here is how it works in a car dealership. Let us assume you and the salesperson have reached a price agreement. The salesperson has to get "approval" from the manager "Bad Guy" to honor his/her agreement with you. However, only the sales manager can accept an offer. The salesperson is a messenger between you and the sales manager.

The next time this strategy is used on you - try this: tell the sales person that you want to go into the sales manager's office together - you want to see how the sales person is going to work for you to get the price you want. They will tell you that is not possible - insist on it.

You can do the same thing when a buyer insists on a lower price. You can call your manager (the bad guy) and report back that the manager was really tough on you, "However, I was able to get the price down a small amount. Not quite what you want, but pretty close." This makes the customer believe you are on their side.

Good guy/bad guy occurs when there are two or more buyers and one is easier to get along with, provides more information, or seems more anxious to make a deal, while the other is more difficult.

Abraham Lincoln's strategy

Abraham Lincoln had a reputation as a lawyer for hardly ever losing a case. His strategy was to unknowingly use the feel/felt/found formula to perfection, however, he probably never heard of it.

Lincoln would never argue or attack an opponent. In fact, Lincoln, at first, would argue his opponent's case telling all the reasons why his opponent was right. He'd appear to agree to all the things his opponent said.

As his opponent was stating his case before the jury, Lincoln would write down everything that was said. Then he would begin changing the minds of the jurors by saying, "We all feel these things are true, and my opponent has skillfully presented them in a way that anyone hearing them would have felt the same, however, there are a few other things that influence this case and when I present them you will find that the way to vote will be obvious."

Then he'd begin slowly with his own arguments. He was a master at diplomacy, at getting people to change their minds and feel good doing it.

Lincoln probably invented the "feel/felt/found formula even though he never heard of it. The feel/felt/found formula can become one of your most valuable tools. Try this response when you get a negative reaction to the price you are presenting or the program you are trying to push through.

"I can certainly understand why you feel the price seems a little high".

"I don't blame you for wanting to get the best value for your money and at the same time keeping your cost down to a minimum."

"Every person I talk to has felt the same as you do when they first looked at the program".

However, after they found out that the small difference in price for the higher quality product was actually the best investment they ever made they saw it from a completely different view."

"Why should I pay you all this money?" This is how I would answer using F/F/F...

"At first glance you are right, it may seem like a large investment. I have served hundreds of clients over the years Bill, and when I first presented my program they also showed a slight concern, just as you are now. Once they realized the amount of value they were receiving in relation to what they were investing, it all made sense. Would you like to review the benefits both to you and your company? For example, how much bottom line profit would a 20% sales increase amount to in actual dollars? Etc."

The key to successfully using this tactic is to try and NOT use the words feel/felt/found, only the structure. It will come off sounding a whole lot more sincere.

Add value to every sale

A sales rep told me how he would go into an account with both a high priced and a low priced product. He would say that he was reluctant to show the higher priced product and said you probably don't want this high quality product. Even though it is the best you can buy, the price is high – much higher than this cheap economy brand. He said that whenever he used this technique the customer seemed to want what the sales person was reluctant to sell.

Another sales rep recently told me a great story about how to keep from giving a discount or from having to negotiate the price. He was having a break job done on his car and the cost was $40. When he asked, "is that the best you can do" here is how he responded: "If you want to negotiate the price – the break job will cost you $50!"

Think about what a great answer that is. What is he really saying? He is saying that I am already giving you the best price I can. He is saying that if you want to negotiate I will raise the price to $50 and we can see if you can get me down to the bottom price of $40.

Reluctance is an important tool that can be used in selling. How? If you give a discount too easily or too quickly you have actually cheated the customer out of the feeling that he or she made a good purchase. Have you ever had the feeling that you paid too much for something? Where did that feeling come from? It came from the fact that the sales person lowered the price too quickly. "Maybe I should have asked for a bigger discount?" You are thinking. "Maybe the sales person has been overcharging me right along?"

A little thought and reluctance actually adds value to the product or service.

I was sitting on the plane and the woman sitting next to me was in advertising sales. When I asked her what the biggest mistake was that she ever made in sales, here is what she told me. "I was calling on a pawn shop with my sales manager. He told me the bottom line price was $1,500 but to try and get $2,000. He said to go down slowly and reluctantly so you "add value" to the program. When the customer asked for the price I made a huge mistake said $1,500! The customer ended up paying $1,400 and I ended up getting chewed out!"

Here is another reason we should be slightly reluctant when giving a price reduction. An accountant once told me that I should forget the term "gross profit" and replace it with "contribution to overhead". He said that every time I lower the price I am giving part of the company away! The warehouse cost is .04%, the sales department cost is .04%, the transportation department is another .04%, administration cost is .04% and the bottom line should be at least .04%. When you cut your price below .20% think about what part of the company you are cutting out and giving away!

You do not want to appear too hungry for the sale or too eager to give everything away. When you do a customer will be suspicious and begin to wonder why you are so anxious to make a sale.

If you give a discount too easily or too quickly you have actually cheated the customer out of the feeling that he or she made a good purchase.

Don't give your lowest price

An experienced buyer will very seldom, if ever, accept your first price. An experienced seller knows this and always presents a price higher than they expect to get.

A buyer will feel like they are not doing their job if they don't get a sales person to move down a little on price. As a seller, if you don't give them a price reduction they will feel like you out-smarted them.

When someone asks you for a price on a single item that you know is price sensitive, try and get them to give you the price they are looking for.

For example: As you start looking up the price or waiting for your computer to boot up, you might respond with: "I'll be happy to give you a price on that, by the way, what price are you looking for?"

If you do get the buyer to tell you how much he or she is willing to pay, act slightly shocked as if their opening price is low!

"I have to admit that price is really low."

When you are selling, always start at your highest price whenever possible. No matter what the customer may say (such as "This is a one-time only offer; take it or leave it!"), don't take it! If they really want to make the purchase, they'll move from that price.

Don't be shy when you state your original price - put on a show of confidence. Amateurs almost always hesitate when giving their first price and professionals very seldom do.

The more you ask for in the beginning, the better. You're not being greedy - you're being smart. Eventually you will meet an acceptable compromise, but usually not in the beginning.

When you ask for a higher price, you can always come down. If you begin by asking for a higher price and you know you will settle for the lower price, everyone comes out a winner. If you start low you may end up having to go ever lower.

Don't be shy when you state your original price - put on a show of confidence. Amateurs almost always hesitate when giving their first price and professionals very seldom do.

Get something in return

Do not keep lowering your price without asking for something in return or you will make it too easy for the buyer to keep asking. The trade off is a very basic yet important strategy when dealing with buyers. Every time you give in to one of the requests such as price reduction, marketing money, extra services, etc., the trade off strategy should go through your mind: "If I do that for the customer, what can I ask the customer to do for me?"

This is our attitude, not our actual statement. Negotiating as a seller is not the same as negotiating as a buyer. If you are selling and you get tough and walk away, at the end of the day you have not sold anything. Most of the negotiating strategies are designed for buyers and must be adjusted if used by a person trying to make a sale.

Many people complain that customers or buyers today have no loyalty. "Show a customer how to save money on a certain item and they will shop around to see if it can be purchased for a few cents cheaper from a competitor." If customers are not loyal, perhaps it is because when you give everything you have, you do not ask for anything in return. Trading builds a relationship. Giving and taking are part of selling; they are part of the process and not a sign of weakness! Here are a few points to keep in mind:

1. Do not assume the customer knows what you want. Make your request loud and clear! Do not be shy about asking for something in return when a customer asks you for a price discount. If it is done in a spirit of cooperation they will not take offence.

2. Whenever you give a price reduction, be sure to ask for something in return. You are not doing anybody favors by giving away something for nothing - the customer will not respect you and you hurt your self respect.

3. Make this an important principle in your selling. Never give up anything without getting something in return (even if what you get seems trivial). The customer offers to buy the floor model of the coffee machine at a reduced price. You, instead of lowering the price, offer a 90-day free service guarantee.

4. The customer requests a lower price on a larger than normal order. You offer some additional marketing support instead.

5. The customer complains that the price is too high. You offer to sell your higher quality product line at a slightly lower price. Explain to the customer that the higher quality is an investment in their customer satisfaction.

6. Whenever lowering the price, never go down in equal increments. If you have an extra five cents built in, go down two cents and if you must go down a second time, reluctantly go down another two cents and a third time use the last penny. Each time you go down on your price ask for an additional line item or something in return.

If customers are not loyal, perhaps it is because when you give everything you have, you do not ask for anything in return. Trading builds a relationship.

Split the difference

As soon as someone suggests splitting the difference, the whole game changes.

The side that makes the offer has essentially revealed what they will settle for. You, a seller, should always let the buyer be the one to offer to split the difference first.

Suppose that after the initial negotiating, you a sales person, have a price of $50 per case on a one thousand case order and the customer wants to pay $45. The buyer says, "Let's split the difference." What they have just done is raised their offer to $47.50.

The negotiating range has changed. Before, the difference was $5. Now the difference is $2.50 per case.

What's your move? Acknowledge the offer with appropriate respect but make it clear that you cannot yet accept because the price is still too low. (Continue to maintain that the top of your limit is $50).

After waiting a few seconds, it becomes your turn to make a counter offer. But now the negotiating range is between $47.50 and $50.00. You say, "Let's meet half-way; I'll come down $1.25 and you come up $1.25."

The deal is struck at $48.75 per case. If you had been the one to offer to split the difference just the opposite might have happened. If you agree to split the difference you would have lowered your price to $47.50.

The buyer would have said to YOU: "Let's meet half-way; I'll come up $1.25 and you come down $1.25. The deal would have been struck at $46.25.

On a one thousand case order the difference would have been $2,500. (Which, of course, would have come out of your gross profit).

The first person who places a value on a product or service establishes its worth.

A perceived value must be established when the customer or buyer makes a low offer gives you a low price, you should counter by presenting an equally high price. This is sometimes referred to as "bracketing."

When the prospect makes a low offer or a sales person presents you with a high price your first reaction should be to "bracket" the price. For example, you are selling a product at $10, you open with $12, the customer is shocked and offers you $8 and you compromise at $10.

Reverse it if you are buying: The sales person offers up a price of $12. You are shocked and offer $8, knowing you will be happy to get it for $10.

The person who offers to split the difference has essentially revealed what they will settle for. You, a seller, should always let the buyer be the one to offer to split the difference first.

Objections: Remove every roadblock to the sale

I have carefully recorded every objection that a customer has presented to me as a reason why they were not interested in buying. My list has all the objections that I have been presented with from a variety of customers and under numerous conditions. Each one of the objections has been researched and I have carefully crafted a response for each one. Not just a canned response, but a real, sincere, well thought out answer based on facts, experience and product knowledge. I am well aware that 67% of most sales are made after 5 objections and I not only anticipate them, but welcome them as a way for the customer to build confidence in me.

My 4% improvement objective:

_____

_____

_____

_____

_____

_____

_____

What the entire book series will do for you

Buying all 13 books is like buying a library of 13 powerful coaching sessions that will increase every skill necessary for generating business. Once you experience the seemingly effortless improvement you will understand why there is a picture of Ben Franklin on every 100 dollar bill.

You will learn how to improve relationships, improve management skills, be more productive, generate more customers, negotiate better contracts, open new accounts, earn more profits and create more sales! Results most people only dream about! If you are a sales professional or an entrepreneur this is the perfect program to boost your sales and increase your profits.

Ben Franklin's system

In our fast paced business and personal life today it has become increasingly difficult to set aside time for self development and improving your skills. With every spare minute taken up by reading blogs, logging on to Facebook, following people on Twitter, responding to text messages and emails and constantly talking on your cell phone, there seems to be little, if any, time left for learning new skills. Even the quiet time behind the wheel of your car is no longer available with satellite radio and cell phone coverage in every corner of the country.

Even though this seems like a new problem, distractions have been around forever. Two hundred years ago a man by the name of Ben Franklin had the same problem. He concluded that it was not a matter of distractions as much as a matter of focus. He set out to solve the problem and created the most effective system for self improvement ever invented.

Ben Franklin gives credit for all his success and accomplishments to the implementation of this system for the success he sought after. Despite being born into a poor family and only receiving two years of formal schooling, Ben Franklin became a successful printer, scientist, musician, author and one of the founding fathers of the United States. Ben Franklin is considered to have been one of the most persuasive and successful people in the history of the United States. He was a very skilled sales person, marketer, negotiator and copywriter. Skills that every business owner, professional person, manager and marketer should have.

In the year 1723, Ben Franklin, at the age of seventeen, arrived in Philadelphia without a penny to his name. At age 42, he retired, wealthy, the first self made millionaire in the country. Few people, before or since have ever been as successful as Benjamin Franklin. He gave credit for his many inventions and business successes to his system for self improvement he created when he was 20 years old.

The key to Franklin's success was his drive to constantly improve himself and accomplish his ambitions. In order to accomplish his goal, Franklin developed and committed himself to a personal improvement program that consisted of mastering 13 principles.

When he was seventy-nine years old, Benjamin Franklin wrote more about this idea than anything else that ever happened to him in his entire life. He felt that he owed all his success and happiness to this one thing. Franklin wrote: "I hope, therefore, that some of my descendants may follow the example and reap the benefit."

Since success is developed by performing small and seemingly insignificant acts, you can use this method by reading and putting into practice the 13 skills that will guarantee your success in sales with scientific certainty.

This program takes advantage of Franklin's system and applies it to improving your skills as a sales professional. This program will show you how to dominate your market by first dominating yourself. By focusing on the 13 skills that make up a highly effective and successful sales professional. As these skills are improved your results and sales increases will also show a dramatic improvement.

The goal of going through the program the first time is to increase each skill by only four percent. With the accomplishment of this small improvement in each skill or attitude your overall improvement will be 52%. Those are results most people only dream about. However, you can accomplish this by investing as little as 45 minutes once a week reading one book and then focusing on improving the single skill during the rest of the week. The second week by reading the second book and focusing on that single skill during the week and so on until all 13 weeks are completed.

You can write the single word on the back of your business card and tape it to your dash board as a reminder. You can put this one word on your smart phone as a reminder as well as on your email signature, your Facebook page or you can even have something worthwhile to tweet about. One word, one week, one skill, one "I am" statement, 4% improvement objective and your subconscious mind will receive the message through all the clutter and act on it.

After the first time through the process you can do as Ben Franklin suggests and go through the program a second, third and fourth time. Get your whole sales team on the same page at the same time and you will experience a whirlwind of new excitement and new business. Or get a like minded colleague and join forces with accountability and focus.

Achieve a 52% improvement

Using Franklin's scientific program for learning your objective is to improve 4% in each area over 13 weeks.

1. Attitude Define what you want and go after it.
2. Respect Earn respect-no more comfort zone.
3. Service Help customers build their business.
4. Urgency Be enthusiastic get things done now.
5. Confidence Remove restrictions and limitations.
6. Persistence Keep going and never give up.
7. Planning Get big results by setting big goals.
8. Questions Ask questions that make the sale.
9. Attention Get attention with irresistible offers.
10. Presenting Give reasons why they should buy.
11. Objections Remove every roadblock to the sale.
12. Closing Ask for the order and get paid.
13. Follow up Remove all hope for competitors.

ATTITUDE
Define what you want and go after it

CONFIDENCE

PRESENTING
Give reasons why they should buy

RESPECT
Earn respect by being an expert

PERSISTENCE

OBJECTIONS
Remove every roadblock to the sale

PLANNING

SERVICE
Help customers build their business

CLOSING
Ask for the order and get paid

QUESTIONS

Ben Franklin's little known scientific

Ben Franklin's little known scientific
formula improves selling skills 52%

URGENCY
Be enthusiastic get things done now

ATTENTION
Make irresistible compelling offers

FOLLOW UP
Remove all hope for competitors

Ben Franklin's little known scientific
formula improves selling skills 52%

Ben Franklin's little known scientific
formula improves selling skills 52%

Ben Franklin's little known scientific
formula improves selling skills 52%

Bob Oros

Bob Oros

Bob Oros

About the author Bob Oros (BobOros.com),

Bob Oros has been a full time speaker and author since 1992 with over 2,000 speaking engagements in all 50 states and several international locations as well as the author of 21 books on sales. Prior to starting his speaking career, Bob served six years in the US Navy as a Communications Specialist and then worked his way from a street sales person to the position of National Sales Manager for a Fortune 200 company.

CSP Award: Bob was awarded the designation of Certified Speaking Professional (CSP) by the National Speakers Association and the International Federation for Professional Speakers. Fewer than 10% of all speakers worldwide qualify for this award.

PWA Member: Bob is a member of the Professional Writers Alliance.

www.ingramcontent.com/pod-product-compliance
Lightning Source LLC
Chambersburg PA
CBHW072248170526
45158CB00003BA/1033